Sign Design
ENVIRONMENTAL
GRAPHICS

Sign Design

ENVIRONMENTAL GRAPHICS

Graphic Design: USA

GRAPHIC *details*

An Imprint of

PBC INTERNATIONAL, INC. ◆ NEW YORK

Distributor to the book trade in the United States and Canada:

Rizzoli International Publications Inc.
300 Park Avenue South
New York, NY 10010

Distributor to the art trade in the United States and Canada:

PBC International, Inc.
One School Street
Glen Cove, NY 11542
1-800-527-2826
Fax 516-676-2738

Distributor throughout the rest of the world:

Hearst Books International
1350 Avenue of the Americas
New York, NY 10019

Library of Congress Cataloging-in-Publication Data

Sign design : environmental graphics / by Graphic Design: USA.
      p.   cm.
    Includes indexes.
    ISBN 0-86636-178-2
    1. Signs and signboards--United States--Lettering.   2. Graphic
arts--United States.   I. Graphic Design: USA (Firm)
    NK3630.3.S64S5   1992   92-5555
    741.6--dc20   CIP

CAVEAT—Information in this text is believed accurate, and will pose
no problem for the student or casual reader. However, the author was
often constrained by information contained in signed release forms,
information that could have been in error or not included at all. Any
misinformation (or lack of information) is the result of failure in these
attestations. The author has done whatever is possible to insure accuracy.

Color separation, printing and binding by
Toppan Printing Co. (H.K.) Ltd. Hong Kong

Typography by
TypeLink, Inc.

Printed in Hong Kong

10 9 8 7 6 5 4 3 2 1

CONTENTS

As designers we are continually faced with the challenge of balancing the utility and beauty of signage. This doesn't mean that every sign has to be bronze letters in a serif typeface design. A flashing neon sign set against an evening sky to alert motorists about an approaching service station is an effective design. The point is that we take the time to consider the best solution for the task at hand.

There is more and more attention devoted to what we as "environmental graphic designers," "signage experts," and "wayfinders" are contributing to communications in the built environment. This book and others like it is evidence of this fact. Increasingly, architects see signage as an integral part of a building and less as a necessary evil. The Society of Environmental Graphic Designers, design publications and architectural journals all provide a forum to examine issues about our profession and how it serves the public.

This is an exciting time for the profession not only as a service business but as a creative force as well. New materials and technologies now extend the limits of what is possible—even accepted as "a sign." Perhaps there will be a time where office buildings come equipped with optional systems for computer generated signs. Wired directly into wall partitions, made of strange composite materials, the system could permit a tenant to install or change a sign from a PC.

Even working with more traditional materials like metal and plastic provides us with creative opportunities, because clients and sign fabricators are more willing to consider new design options. The possibility of the signs to become more ornamental in the absence of art is increasing. Signs which are more "architectural" in scale are taking the place of plaques on the wall. The application of messages, the manipulation of materials and methods of installation are being inventively explored by designers working on large and small scale projects.

One of the greatest challenges that faces designers in the future will be to achieve the same success we have experienced for design-aware clients in the private sector, as for those less enlightened ones in the public sector. This is not an easy assignment and it takes a courageous soul to enter this arena. I applaud those who have already done so.

Perhaps the same theories that work for well-designed sign programs for museums, corporate offices, retail plazas and airports can be taken to the street. Beginning with "design by subtraction," maybe some of the visual clutter can be reduced and information effectively organized for clearer communication.

With this as a foundation for positive change, the imagination and creative skill of environmental graphic designers will greatly benefit the world around us.

Kenneth Carbone
Carbone Smolan Associates

FOREWORD

Herbert M. Meyers

© Harry Heleotis

David Gibson

Joshua S. Marcus

Design and diversity are the dual themes of *Sign Design: Environmental Graphics*. The importance of design in the sign process is a primary focus of the book because the sign industry is becoming increasingly designer-driven—rather than manufacturer led—as the '90s unfold. The reason for this trend is as straightforward as it is significant: 'design' in its many manifestations and disciplines is coming of age as business and society gradually recognize the potential of 'good design' to enrich the quality of life and visual environment, to inform and communicate, to enhance products and performance, and to generate economic development in a time of intense clutter and brutal economic competition. Design is a powerful force in commerce and culture, and that message is getting through to a broader spectrum of private and public decision-makers.

To assure a cross section of well-designed signs, we solicited current examples of sign excellence from graphic design firms, corporations, architects and advertising agencies around the country. From the thousands of possibilities, selections for inclusion in the book were made by an internationally-known panel of graphic design, sign design, and identity specialists: Herbert M. Meyers of Gerstman + Meyers, whose firm employs over 50 design and marketing employees and whose client roster includes Kraft, Purdue, Quaker Oats, Omni Hotels, Nabisco, Johnson & Johnson, to name a few; David Gibson, president of the Society of Environmental

Graphic Designers and founding principal of Two Twelve Associates whose current projects include environmental graphic standards for the Boston Central Artery Highway and Tunnel Project, the South Street Seaport, the Baltimore Harbor Promenade and the Baltimore Light Rail system; Heide Mohrmann-Tidwell, design director, Peterson & Blyth Associates whose recent corporate identity and packaging clients have included Richardson-Vicks, S.C. Johnson, Drackett and Chattem; and Joshua S. Marcus of PAOS New York which provides corporate identity consulting to an international clientele including Mazda, Kenwood, Bridgestone, Kirin Brewery, Ricoh, Sumitomo Bank, NTT and Kawasaki Steel. Ken Carbone of architectural sign fame—his Carbone Smolan firm recently completed the new sign system at the Louvre in Paris—provides perspective in his Foreword. The result is a compilation of nearly 500 photographs of state-of-the-art signs and sign systems with a heavy emphasis on design excellence, intelligence and sophistication.

The second theme of the book is diversity. Signs are everywhere—in the stores where we shop, the buildings in which we live, the streets that we travel, the offices where we work, the public facilities we share. It is that very diversity which raises the true design challenge for signage experts: to solve design problems on a case-by-case basis in an almost limitless range of real-world environments. For that reason, we have tried to include a broad range of signs and sign systems that display successful solutions in a variety of visual environments. These include restaurants, shopping malls, parks, hotels, office and government buildings, convention centers, hospitals, libraries, zoos, golf clubs, and much, much more. Located throughout the United States, the projects presented are as diverse as the Kennedy Center, Team Disney, Southland Mall, Carnegie Hall, Salt Lake City-County Building, Oak Park Hospital, Mizner Park, Jungle of the Apes, Hollywood Roosevelt Hotel, Blackhawk Grille, Rockefeller Center, Tampa Convention Center and the Ronald Reagan Presidential Library.

Signs provide vital functions in our lives, providing identification, orientation, information, direction and decoration. One need only glance around the office or the street to know that most signs fail to meet some or all of those important goals, and that is disheartening. On the other hand, there are powerful economic and aesthetic forces—as well as an array of tough and talented designers—that are driving up the signing standards for all of us and providing optimism that the '90s will be a watershed period in effective sign design on a broad scale.

The examples in *Sign Design: Environmental Graphics* demonstrate that the basis for optimism is real.

Gordon Kaye
Graphic Design: USA

Business/Corporate Identity

CHAPTER ONE

Team Disney East Coast Headquarters

CLIENT:
Team Disney
Orlando, Florida
DESIGN FIRM:
Tracy Turner Design, Inc.
ARCHITECTS:
Arata Isozaki and Associates
FABRICATOR:
McCurdy Shea

The designers kept all of the graphics in black and white and used the "Mickey" ear as a predominant and repetitive design motif for the new East Coast headquarters in over 600,000 square feet of office space.

For the largest sundial in the world, the designers developed an explanation graphically of how the sundial works and came up with the idea of putting quotations about time in black granite circles in the circular paving within the court.

Imprimis Technology, Inc.

CLIENT:
    Imprimis Technology, Inc.
DESIGNER:
    Tim Larsen
DESIGN FIRM:
    Larsen Design Office
FABRICATOR:
    Nordquist Sign Company

These exterior signs are components of a new corporate logo fabricated in bold white lettering. The red accent and white lettering are unifying elements appearing throughout the signage program.

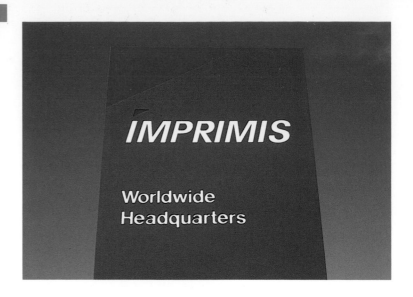

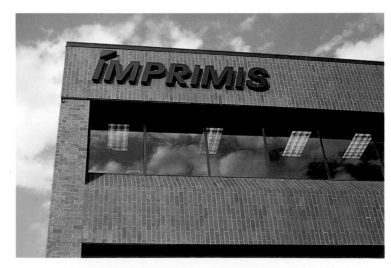

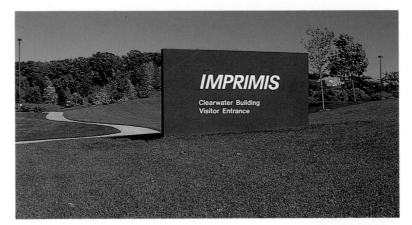

Nike World Headquarters and The Joe Paterno Child Development Center

CLIENT:
Nike, Inc.
Beaverton, Oregon
DESIGN DIRECTOR:
Kenneth G. Ambrosini
PROJECT MANAGER:
Richard A. Gottfried
DESIGNERS:
Eric Knudston, Dardinelle Troen
Todd Lasher, Lewellyn Seibold
DESIGN FIRM:
Design Partnership
ARCHITECT:
Thompson Vaivoda & Associates
INTERIOR DESIGNER:
Wyatt Stapper Architects
PHOTOGRAPHERS:
Design Partnership, Robert Graves Photography
Strode Eckert Photography, Todd Eckelman
Photography

"Just Do It," the advertising slogan for Nike, the international footwear and apparel company, became the the philosophy for their signage program. Design Partnership was given the task to solve the exterior and interior wayfinding and identification program for Nike's new world campus in Beaverton, Oregon. The designers were to provide a workable solution that not only functioned, but at the same time would disappear when not needed. Signage played-off of materials and conditions found throughout the interiors and interior architecture; perforated metals, laminated "rice paper" glass, high-tech fasteners, play of light and shadow, and the influence of the Far East as conveyed by the use of grided furnishings and shoji-like skylights.

THE MIKE SCHMIDT BUILDING
THE MICHAEL JORDAN BUILDING
THE JOAN BENOIT SAMUELSON CENTER
<

BOWERMAN DRIVE
STEVE PREFONTAINE HALL
THE DAN FOUTS BUILDING
THE ALBERTO SALAZAR BUILDING
THE JOHN McENROE BUILDING
>

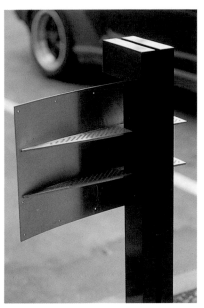

RECEPTION
CENTER
>

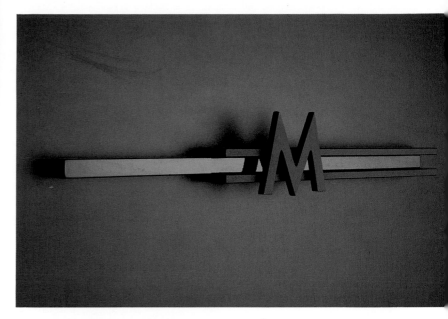

CHERYL ESON

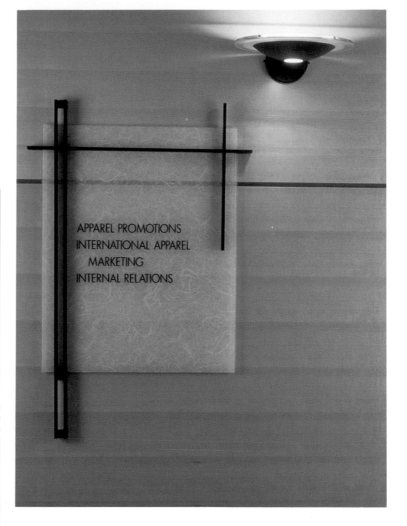

APPAREL PROMOTIONS
INTERNATIONAL APPAREL
MARKETING
INTERNAL RELATIONS

SALAD BAR
CREATE YOUR SALAD
FROM OUR SELECTION OF GREENS
FRESH VEGETABLES TOPPINGS
& QUALITY DRESSINGS
.20
PER OUNCE

Form and function, underlying Nike's synthesis of their product line manifested itself in the design for the regulatory signage sites. Both the "stop" and "caution" signage were designed to allow the headlamps of approaching vehicles to illuminate the message.

In the signage program for the Nike's Day Care facility, "The Joe Paterno Child Development Center," the circle and triangle were selected as the design direction and theme for identifying the signs and desk bar. It seemed appropriate since those shapes are "building blocks" in a child's first exposure to learning.

The materials used were durable and able to withstand potential abuse since Nike's educational philosophy was "hands-on" and the locations of the signs were at hands height. Plaques were epoxy coated silk-screened graphics applied to a metal substrate. The purpose of marking the glass was to provide warning and to increase vocabulary and pronunciation skills.

The desk bar was painted metal with changeable glass panels. The names were marked with removable vinyl die-cut letters. This responded to Nike's requirement to identify the individuals and to address the multiple roles of the director, educators and support staff.

ABC's of Broadcasting

CLIENT:
  Capital Cities/ABC, Inc.
  New York City
DESIGN FIRM:
  Barry Brothers
FABRICATORS:
  Barry Brothers and EverGreene Painting Studio
MATERIALS:
  Flash Vinyl Acrylic Paint, canvas

The ABC's of Broadcasting is a triptych mural created in 1985-86 for the Broadcast Operations Complex of The American Broadcasting Company, Inc. The murals are on permanent display at 47 West 66th Street in New York City. The semi-abstract design is built by utilizing the shapes and colors of equipment found in television production facilities and used by television production and broadcast engineers.

Herman Miller Pavilion

CLIENT:
  Herman Miller
DESIGNERS:
  **Michael Donovan, Eileen Boxer, Dana Christensen,
  Gwen Wilkins**
DESIGN FIRM:
  Donovan & Green
FABRICATOR:
  Displaymakers
PHOTOGRAPHER:
  Nick Merrick of Hedrich Blessing
MATERIALS:
  **Projected light patterns, photographic reproduction,
  silkscreening**

In the Herman Miller Pavilion, the multi-tiered space allows for all of Herman Miller's seating to be on display at
once. Theatrical lighting fixtures that project graphics,
patterns and colors can be changed easily. In the product display area, the rotated structure was inserted in
the large open space to create scale and a sense of place
for the more intimate product. Freestanding graphic
exhibit panels convey specific product and program
information.

Oasis Laundries, Inc.

CLIENT:
Oasis Laundries, Inc.
DESIGNERS:
Rick Tharp, Karen Kimi Nomura, Kim Tomlinson
DESIGN FIRM:
THARP DID IT
FABRICATOR:
SignTech
INTERIOR DESIGN:
John Mathamas

The Oasis Laundry is a franchise operation. Each location features coin-operated laundry equipment, a big screen TV, a juice and snack bar and, of course, restrooms. The interior signage was meant to be entertaining as well as instructional. The pyramid-shaped fasteners were custom designed to hold the signs away from the wall to give an added dimension. All interior signage was silk-screened onto the back of clear Plexiglas.

Heritage International Gallery

CLIENT:
   Heritage International Gallery
DESIGNERS:
   Dominic Pangborn, Han Kim
DESIGN FIRM:
   Pangborn Design, Ltd.
FABRICATOR:
   Casey Sign Company
PHOTOGRAPHER:
   Gordon Alexander

Each piece of artwork has a heritage of its own in the Heritage International Gallery. The signage illustrates this philosophy throughout the design. Red and green is used to symbolize the East/West balance of the gallery. The heritage of the gallery itself is brought out into the forefront of the signage through the use of the Pangborn crest.

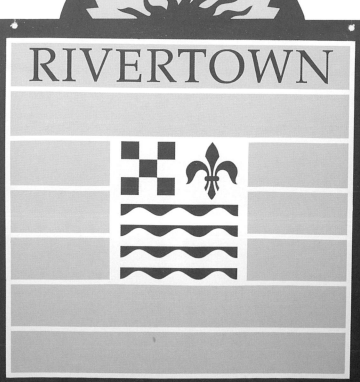

Rivertown Business Association

CLIENT:
   Rivertown Business Association
DESIGNERS:
   Dominic Pangborn, Han Kim
DESIGN FIRM:
   Pangborn Design, Ltd.
FABRICATOR:
   Casey Sign Company
PHOTOGRAPHER:
   Gordon Alexander
MATERIALS:
   Aluminum, enamel paint

The signs were installed around the perimeter of Detroit's historic Rivertown area in order to bring awareness to the area and Association. The new signage has brought about strong appeal and recognition in the community.

Corning Corporate Headquarters Exhibition/Signage

CLIENT:
   Corning Corporate Headquarters
DESIGNERS:
   Michael Donovan, Allen Wilpon
DESIGN FIRM:
   Donovan & Green
FABRICATOR:
   Maltbie Associates
PHOTOGRAPHER:
   Wolfgang Hoyt
MATERIALS:
   Dichroic filters, prisms, optical mirrors, glass

The designers wanted to produce a visceral entry experience that also told a story about the client. In the 1850s, Corning Glass Works moved to Corning, New York, to manufacture red and green glass lenses for railroad signal lights. A century-and-a-half later, the altered transmission of light became a major component of Corning's business. Because light is a consistent element the company has always been involved with, the designers chose to use light as the key ingredient in their signage program.

Using dichroic filters, prisms and optical mirrors, a pure white light was focused on a 50′ wall which created a changing pattern of spectral light. Dichroic filters separate light into the various colors of the visible light spectrum. By carefully selecting dichroic filters and aiming them through mirrors and prisms, the color palette becomes an ever-changing array. Light sources were programmed by computer so that over the course of the day the visual presentation constantly changed.

Editel

CLIENT:
Editel
DESIGNER:
Linda Konda
DESIGN FIRM:
Clifford Selbert Design
FABRICATOR:
Design Communications
PHOTOGRAPHER:
Anton Grassl

Using elements from the corporate logo, the designer illuminated the exterior identity sign for a video production company with two light pipes, one in a horizontal position and the other positioned vertically.

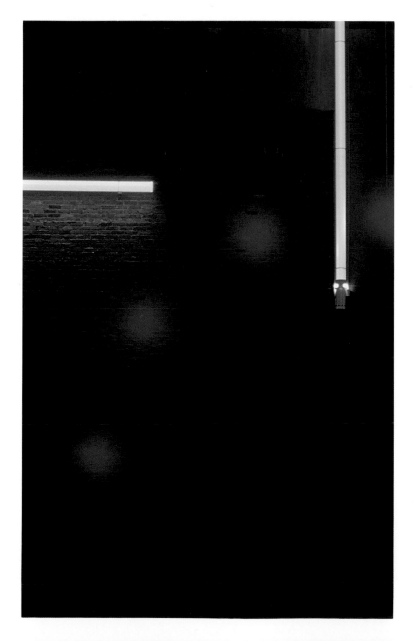

Republic National Bank

CLIENT:
Republic National Bank
DESIGNER:
Michael Donovan
DESIGN FIRM:
Donovan & Green
FABRICATOR:
The Other Sign Company
MATERIALS:
Banner fabric, painted plywood

The construction barricade on Fifth Avenue was designed to have a festive quality. The colors of the banners changed to reflect the seasons. In this way, the bank's image and presence during construction was kept lively and interesting.

American Isuzu Motors, Inc.

CLIENT:
  American Isuzu Motors, Inc.
CREATIVE DIRECTOR:
  Dale Hoover
DESIGNERS:
  Jacqui Ghosin, Anthony Luk, Joe Harvard
DESIGN FIRM:
  Addison Design Consultants
FABRICATOR:
  Zimmerman Sign Company
MATERIALS:
  Steel supports, aluminum clading and cans, acrylic faces, internal illumination

The designers found that the original "twin towers" symbol was recognizable and that it signified the distinguished quality of Japanese automotive products. They showcased the towers within an ellipse, accenting a new logotype that is unique, bold and technology-driven. The corporate version of the new identity makes exclusive use of Isuzu's proprietary red. The dealer version is more promotional; red creates a dramatic beacon effect while the grey suggests a machine-driven ruggedness. The sign, monolithic in structure, is unmistakable along the cluttered boulevards of Auto row.

DuPont

CLIENT:
  DuPont
DESIGNERS:
  Mike Quon, Eileen Kinneary
DESIGN FIRM:
  Mike Quon Design Office
PHOTOGRAPHER:
  Mike Quon

This sign was designed for the yearly National Pro-Cycling Championships Racing Event.

Real Estate/Building Identification

CHAPTER TWO

"1000 Broadway"

CLIENT:
Hillman Properties N.W.
Portland, Oregon
PROJECT MANAGER:
Richard A. Gottfried
DESIGN DIRECTOR:
Kenneth G. Ambrosini
DESIGNER:
Lewellyn Seibold
DESIGN FIRM:
Design Partnership
ARCHITECT:
BOOR/A Architects

The overall design for the 24-story "1000 Broadway" office building plays off the history of the old Broadway movie house while incorporating a neo-classical style. The 55-foot sculpture serves as the building identifier and as the marque for the four movie theatres located in the building. The identifier is constructed of painted steel accented with stainless steel cables and clevis pins. Exposed neon progressively and rhythmically spells out "Broadway."

The exterior identification consists of the building address at the main entry and parking identification. The building address is of flat cut-out stainless steel numerals laminated to cut-out acrylic, with sandblasted returns protruding through a muntz metal fascia. The address is internally illuminated.

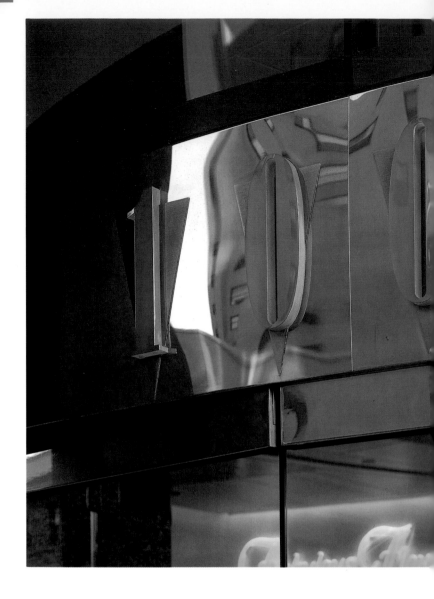

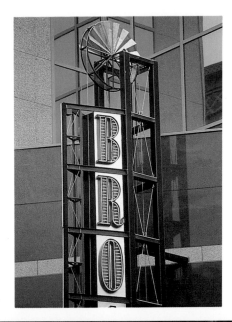

The lobby directory is a free-floating two piece glass design with a photographic film positive sandwiched between the face and back plates. The entire unit floats 2½" off the neoprene glass wall. It is illuminated by the ceiling cove lighting element and is supported by bolts contained within the polished brass fasteners to wood blocking located within the wall. The face plates and the entire unit are removable by unscrewing the fastener button heads.

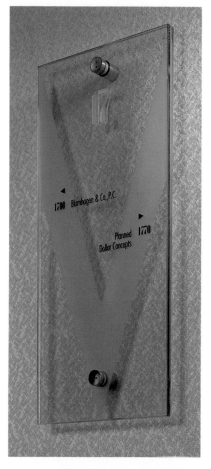

The parking identifier is a play of symbology and color. The international symbol for parking is illuminated white when parking is available and the background illuminates red when the facility is full. The materials are neon, perforated stainless steel and painted steel.

Norwest Center

CLIENT:
   Cesar Pelli & Associates Architects
DESIGNERS:
   Chris Calori, Peter Harrison
DESIGN FIRM:
   Calori & Vanden-Eynden, Ltd.
FABRICATORS:
   Exterior identification by Metallic Arts
   Illuminated elevator signs by Spencor
MATERIALS:
   Bronze

The designers used cast bronze prismatic letters and horizontal bronze bars, along with historical cast bronze medallions salvaged from the original building to create a contemporary version of classic art deco architectural signage.

Worldwide Plaza

CLIENT:
  Worldwide Plaza
DESIGNERS:
  Michael Donovan, Susan Berman, Alexis Cohen, Robert Henry, Lori Hom
DESIGN FIRM:
  Donovan & Green
FABRICATOR:
  Signs + Decals Corporation
ARCHITECTS:
  Skidmore, Owings & Merrill
PHOTOGRAPHER:
  Austin Hughes
MATERIALS:
  Etched and filled bronze, glass, plexiglass, silkscreening

Worldwide Plaza occupies four acres between Eighth and Ninth Avenues, 49th and 50th Streets in New York City. It is a mixed-use commercial and residential development with retail space and off-street parking. A 49-story, 1.5 million square foot skyscraper is located along the Eighth Avenue portion of the site, stepping down to lower housing on the Ninth Avenue portion—with an unusually large, landscaped mid-block plaza and drive-through. Donovan and Green developed the entire signage program, including office tower signage, plaza signage, residential signage and standards for application, and public parking signage.

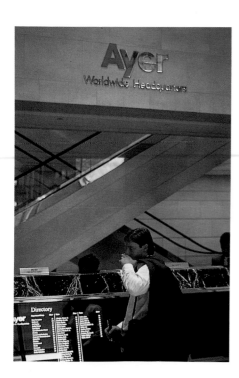

Rockefeller Center

CLIENT:
Rockefeller Center
New York City
DESIGNERS:
Michael Donovan, Eileen Boxer, Louis Scrima
DESIGN FIRM:
Donovan & Green
FABRICATOR:
The Other Sign Company
MATERIALS:
Brass, glass, plexiglass

Rockefeller Center, above and below ground, covers approximately 12 square blocks in the center of Manhattan. The designers' challenge was to create a complex informational system to guide people who have no reference points through a maze of restaurants, shops, office buildings, entertainment facilities, and key public transportation stations. The signage had to intelligently instruct and be aesthetically appropriate to the landmark's art deco architecture. The system includes all directional, continual direction signs, public amenities information, and all retail signs and retail storefronts.

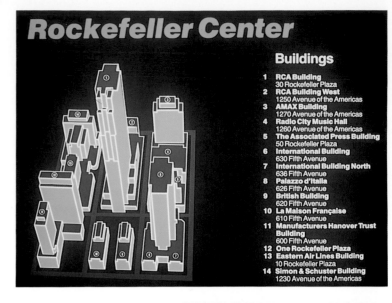

Rockefeller Center

Buildings

1. **RCA Building**
   30 Rockefeller Plaza
2. **RCA Building West**
   1250 Avenue of the Americas
3. **AMAX Building**
   1270 Avenue of the Americas
4. **Radio City Music Hall**
   1260 Avenue of the Americas
5. **The Associated Press Building**
   50 Rockefeller Plaza
6. **International Building**
   630 Fifth Avenue
7. **International Building North**
   636 Fifth Avenue
8. **Palazzo d'Italia**
   626 Fifth Avenue
9. **British Building**
   620 Fifth Avenue
10. **La Maison Française**
    610 Fifth Avenue
11. **Manufacturers Hanover Trust Building**
    600 Fifth Avenue
12. **One Rockefeller Plaza**
13. **Eastern Air Lines Building**
    10 Rockefeller Plaza
14. **Simon & Schuster Building**
    1230 Avenue of the Americas

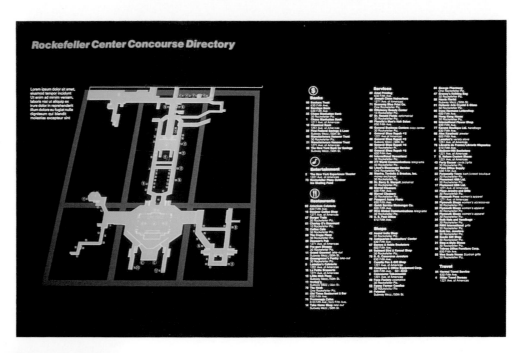

City and County Building

CLIENT:
City and County Building on Washington Square
Salt Lake City, Utah
PRINCIPAL DESIGNER:
Rebecca Jacoby
DESIGN FIRM:
Jacoby-Reese Design
ARCHITECTS:
Robert Jacoby Architect & Associates
FABRICATOR:
Granite Mill
Exterior cast iron signs by ASI Signs
PHOTOGRAPHERS:
Scott Tanner, Jan Schout, Rebecca Jacoby

The interior signs integrate the restored materials of the project, contribute to the historic design characteristics and create a functional, legible and changeable sign system. The designers created a sign system that was inspired by the "Eastlake" geometrical Renaissance revival form patterns. They used solid oak frames to relate to existing wood details and brass, granite, gold porcelain enamel medallions and incised graphic processes to create sign components for the interior public spaces of the building. A related design incorporating cast iron, porcelain enamel and original J.L. Mott cast patterns from 1880 were used for the exterior site.

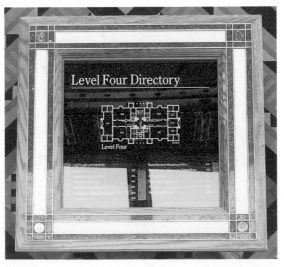

Office of the Mayor
Community Affairs

245

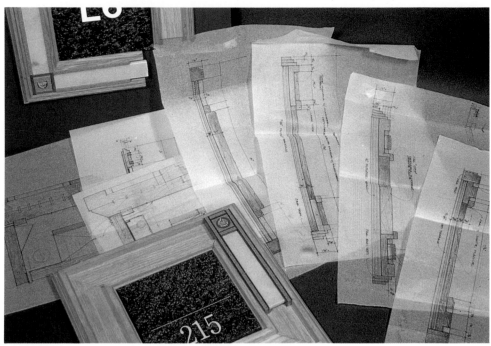

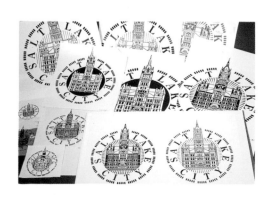

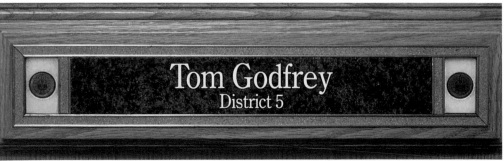

Tom Godfrey
District 5

New York University Dormitory

CLIENT:
New York University
DESIGNERS:
Chris Calori, Brenda Sisson
DESIGN FIRM:
Calori & Vanden-Eynden, Ltd.
FABRICATOR:
Letteragraphics
PHOTOGRAPHER:
Elliott Kaufman
MATERIALS:
Distressed aluminum, abrasion-resistant acrylic, tamper-proof mechanical fasteners, fluorescent lighting

The designers focused on solving problems of sign vandalism, theft, maintenance and reinforcing the building's post-modern architectural vein.

City of Crystal Lake

CLIENT:
City of Crystal Lake
Crystal Lake, Illinois
DESIGN FIRM:
PlanCom, Inc.
FABRICATOR:
ASI Sign Systems/Chicago
MATERIAL:
Aluminum

The City of Crystal Lake, Illinois, held a design competition to create an architectural sign system for their new public building. The site is a 4-acre property with multiple building entrances as well as several vehicular traffic patterns within the grounds. The design theme of the system was derived from the strong architectural details of the main entrance. The burgundy color was derived from an accent color in the bricks.

Tallyrand Office Park

CLIENT:
Robert Martin Company
DESIGN FIRM:
Carbone Smolan Associates
PHOTOGRAPHER:
Richard Marin

This exterior sign/sculpture is composed of T-shaped panels which graduate in color from green to blue or blue to green depending on the direction from which you approach the sign. They are fabricated out of painted aluminum with internal steel framing.

2015 Main Street

CLIENT:
2015 Main Street
DESIGNERS:
Kenneth Carbone, Beth Bangor
DESIGN FIRM:
Carbone Smolan Associates
PHOTOGRAPHER:
Kenneth Carbone

The 2015 Main Street sign/sculpture was fabricated out of one 4′ × 8′ sheet of aluminum.

Royal Executive Park

CLIENT:
London & Leeds Corporation
DESIGNERS:
David Vanden-Eynden, Julie Vogel
DESIGN FIRM:
Calori & Vanden-Eynden, Ltd.
FABRICATOR:
Signs + Decals Corporation
PHOTOGRAPHER:
James R. Morse

The designers developed a sign program that would provide color and atmosphere to an existing six-building office park complex. Old signs were recycled and incorporated into the new system. Permanence of banner signs was key to keeping long-term maintenance costs down.

Hills Plaza

CLIENT:
Beta West
DESIGNER:
Tom Fairclough
DESIGN FIRM:
Primo Angeli Inc.
CREATIVE DIRECTOR:
Primo Angeli

Hills Plaza is a mixed-use development along the Embarcadero Waterfront in San Francisco. Primo Angeli's scope of work includes programming, thematic design development and implementation of all exterior and interior environmental graphics and signage. The project includes 40,000 square feet of retail, two office towers totalling 550,000 square feet and 85 residential condominiums.

Landmark Centre

CLIENT:
Landmarks Group
Atlanta, Georgia
DESIGNER:
Leigh M. Young
ARCHITECTS:
Alfonso Architects
Tampa, Florida
PHOTOGRAPHER:
Gary Resnick
ADVERTISING FIRM:
Clint Cline—Creative Director

The Landmark Centre sign has neon lit ziggurats to match the wedding cake at the top of the 36-story building.

Citicorp Center

CLIENT:
Citicorp
DESIGNER:
Kenneth Carbone
DESIGN FIRM:
Carbone Smolan Associates
PHOTOGRAPHER:
Kenneth Carbone

This 24' long "canopy-like" sign is cantilevered off the building facade. Ten triangular-shaped panels give the sign visual impact without added weight and stress on the building. Each panel is fabricated out of perforated aluminum and is finished in automotive paint.

Prudential Center

CLIENT:
**The Prudential Property Company
Boston, Massachusetts**
DESIGN FIRM:
Communication Arts Inc.
ARCHITECTS:
Sikes Jenning Kelly & Brewer

The designers created the signage and graphics program for the parking garage, entries, common area amenities, custom light fixtures, retail arcades, storefronts and the project identity.

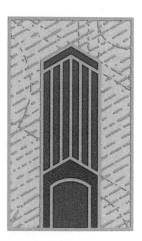

PRUDENTIAL
CENTER
BOSTON

One East River Place Billboard

CLIENT:
Solow Building Company
DESIGNERS:
Michael Donovan, Susan Berman, Robert Henry
DESIGN FIRM:
Donovan & Green
FABRICATOR:
Rathe Productions
MATERIALS:
Painted plywood, scotchcal vinyl graphics, rear-lit duratrans
PHOTOGRAPHER:
Austin Hughes

To communicate the project identity of the 50-story One East River Place, the Solow Building Company needed a sign for motorists passing by the luxury residence under construction. Using simple, easy-to-read typography and bold colors, they created a sort of "kinetic flipbook" for motorists. The faster a driver approaches the sign—up to 50 mph—the more exciting and effective it is.

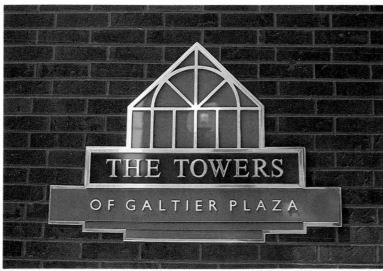

Galtier Plaza

CLIENT:
Galtier Plaza
DESIGNER:
Tim Larsen
DESIGN FIRM:
Larsen Design Office
FABRICATOR:
Serigraphics Sign Systems

Identification signage of the apartment building element of a large office, retail and apartment complex.

Retail/Shopping Centers

CHAPTER THREE

Mizner Park

CLIENT:
Crocker & Company
DESIGN FIRM:
Tracy Turner Design, Inc.
ARCHITECTS:
Cooper, Carry and Associates

The designers developed a comprehensive signage and graphics program for this $75 million mixed-use commercial and residential town center development in Boca Raton, Florida. In addition, they developed a color system for the storefronts and railings, selected the colors and patterns for the awnings, established a tenant graphics, and selected building and window colors.

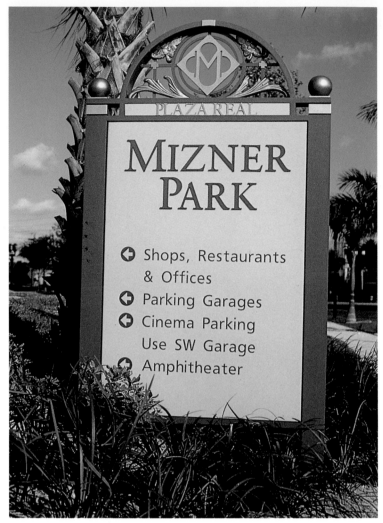

Jordano's Kitchen Supply

CLIENT:
Jordano's Kitchen Supply
Santa Barbara, California
DESIGNERS:
Jack R. Biesek, Jennifer Davis
DESIGN FIRM:
Biesek Design
FABRICATOR:
Painting by Jeff Hauz
Lettering by Sharp Sign Company
PHOTOGRAPHER:
Joseph Kasparowitz

Signs and graphics were designed to complement the interior architecture and the theme reflects the Mediterranean style of this culinary store. Using the hand painted trompe l'oeil technique and faux finishes, the designers created the illusion of a stone archway.

The Mall of Memphis

CLIENT:
The Hahn Company
San Diego, California
DESIGN FIRM:
Farrington Design Group
FABRICATOR:
Nordquist Sign Company
PHOTOGRAPHER:
Chris Hamilton

The overall theme of the signage program for The Mall of Memphis exterior was the introduction of a large "M" letterform. Four new mall entrance portals, constructed in varying patterns of split-faced blocks with accent grids of glazed and glass blocks, were shaped and sized differently to assist shoppers in remembering their parking locations. Vibrantly colored exterior logos, illuminated with white halo lighting, intersect an overscaled metal "M" and mark each portal.

Interior signage, such as custom designed directories and unusually shaped informational/directional signs help shoppers navigate the center's two levels and four entries. A banner program was developed to complement light poles that were installed to bring light to the core of the mall.

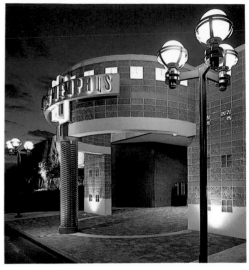

Fashion Island

CLIENT:
Irvine Company
DESIGNER:
Noel Davies
DESIGN FIRM:
Davies Associates
FABRICATOR:
Hampton Associates

The graphics program was part of the overall renaissance of Fashion Island, an existing shopping center in Newport Beach, California. The program consists of entrance signage, district identification elements, tenant identification, parking signage and decorative banners.

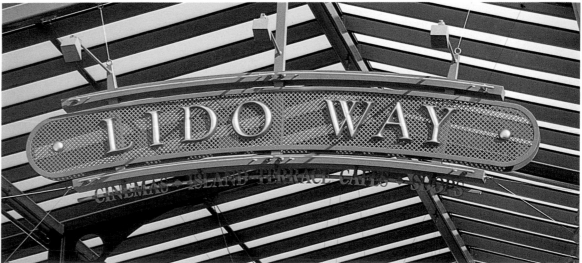

Gurnee Mills

CLIENT:
**Western Development Corporation
Washington, D.C.**
DESIGN PRINCIPAL:
Henry Beer
DESIGNERS:
**Bryan Gough, Paul Mack,
Larry Weeks, Lydia Young**
DESIGN FIRM:
Communication Arts Inc.
PROJECT DIRECTOR:
John Ward
ARCHITECT:
Cambridge Seven Associates
PHOTOGRAPHER:
R. Greg Hursley

Located midway between Chicago and Milwaukee, this new, 2-million-square-foot outlet mall is the world's largest. Every detail at Gurnee Mills is referential to the American Midwest. The Dine-O-Rama food court takes its inspiration from old cars and America's love affair with automobiles, while the rotation sign at Lake County Fare was inspired by the midwestern tradition of the summer state fair. Banquettes in Dine-O-Rama were custom-made to resemble car seats, and the ceiling was painted and lighted to give an evening sky effect. The food court tenant storefronts were designed to be reminiscent of road side food stands of times gone by, complete with suspended clouds and billboards.

Willowbrook Mall

CLIENT:
The Rouse Company
DESIGNERS:
Reginald Wade Richey, Karl Hirschmann
DESIGN FIRM:
The Office of Reginald Wade Richey
ARCHITECTS:
Cope Linder Architects
FABRICATOR:
Zimmerman Metals
MATERIALS:
Painted metal pylons, arcs, lasercut aluminum letters

The designers created the center's graphic identity, signage and special lighting and established architectural graphic criteria for Willowbrook, a retail center in Wayne, New Jersey. All signage and special lighting forms were derived from the falling water arcs of the center's graphic identity. Swans swimming upon a watery "W" are the central element of the food court signage at the Willowbrook Mall.

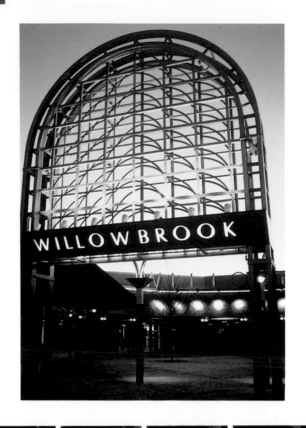

Lee Point-of-Sale System

CLIENT:
Bassett Walker
DESIGNERS:
Program Manager: **Jaimie Alexander,**
Design Team: **Paul Lechleiter, Sandy McKissick,
Paul Westrick, Wendie Wulff**
DESIGN FIRM:
Fitch RichardsonSmith
FABRICATOR:
Tim Serra & Associates and Design Concepts, Inc.
PHOTOGRAPHERS:
Philip Porcella, Mark A. Steele
MATERIALS:
**Wood sign holders and wood panels: Natural beech
Banners: Tyvek with wooden dowels
Posters: Coronado SIST 80# cover
POS signs: Offset printed/mounted on SBS**

This point-of-sale system for Lee sweats, jerseys, and tees was developed to explain the product offering to the retail consumer and to organize, display and enhance the garments.

Lee Brand Room

CLIENT:
The Lee Company
DESIGNERS:
Program Manager: **Jaimie Alexander**
Design Team: **Paul Lechleiter, Kelly Mooney, Paul Westrick**
DESIGN FIRM:
Fitch RichardsonSmith
FABRICATOR:
Robert Propst and Columbus Sign Co.
MATERIALS:
Fiberglas, wood, gatorfoam, applied photography, vinyl letters, silk-screen

One primary design objective for the brand room was to create impact and visual interest in every information module. The freestanding wall provides information on Lee's marketing capabilities on one side, while displaying shelved products on the other side. The wall is composed of a fiberglass back panel sandwiched between maple uprights. An exposed metal structure separates fiberglass panels at the front and the rear. Photos are mounted to sentra and then to fiberglass.

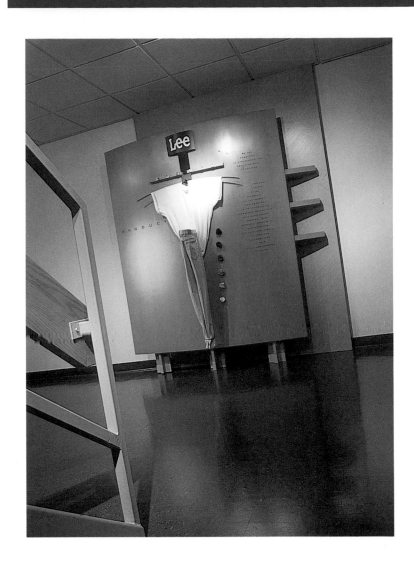

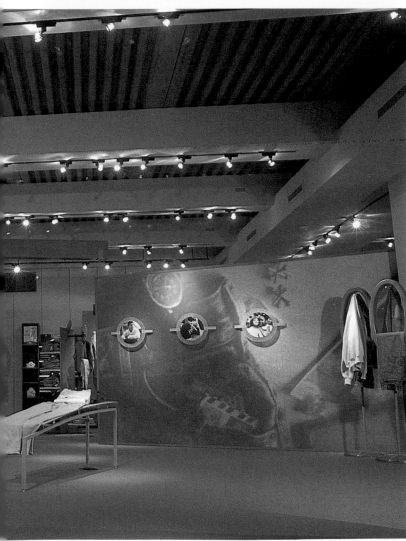

Santa Monica Place

CLIENT:
**The Rouse Company
Columbia, Maryland**
DESIGN PRINCIPAL:
Richard Foy
DESIGNERS:
Mike Doyle, Paul Mack, Keith Harley
PROJECT DIRECTOR:
John Ward
DESIGN FIRM:
Communication Arts Inc.
ARCHITECT:
Ray Bailey Architects
PHOTOGRAPHERS:
Jerry Butts, R. Greg Hursley

In the renovation of the retail center, Santa Monica Place in Santa Monica, California, Communication Arts designed the exterior entries, interior architecture, food court, project signage and common area amenities. The firm added bold signage, accent lighting and light fixtures. To increase public awareness of Santa Monica Place, the remodeled entries were accentuated with architectural forms, signs and colors. Inside, the designers enlarged the food court area to form a focal point anchor to the new entertainment mall. The food court sign, "Eatz" is vandal-proof and easy to maintain.

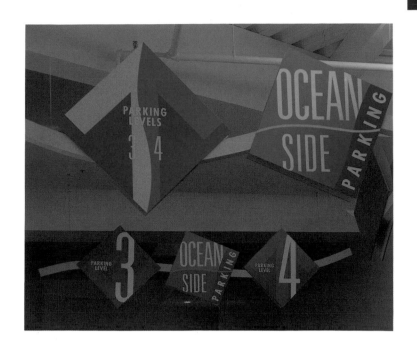

Union Station

CLIENT:
Union Station
Indianapolis, Indiana
DESIGNER:
Tony L. Horton
DESIGN FIRM:
T L Horton Design, Inc.
MANAGEMENT FIRM:
Moor + South
FABRICATOR:
T L Horton Design, Inc
PHOTOGRAPHER:
Joe Aker/Aker Photography

The designer implements a colorful train motif in the signage system to complement the 100-year-old historical station and to guide the visitor through the retail center. The Union Station sign over the stairway indicates access to more shopping downstairs and further identifies the existing food court area. The sign is two sided with neon letters identifying the food court and restaurants. The train, the center's symbol, was silk screened in four colors and was applied to the top of the sign.

The 9'8" high freestanding double-sided directory features all stores and shops in a backlit floorplan and a keyed store directory correlated to the locator map. The logo is dimensional and applied to the arched top. The sign's added feature as a shopping bag dispenser, adds to its resources for the shopper.

Train conductors were cut out of MDF and made to freestand throughout the retail area of the center. The colorful signs, silk screened with ten colors stand six feet high and identify additional shops and directories to the other areas of the mixed use complex—hotel, food court, offices and restaurants. Also in view are the retail blade signs, 36″×52″. Each sign with the trackside logo is applied to simulated crossing signs. The fiberwood signs, silk screened are suspended from painted metal poles with ribbon-like bent sheet metal.

Beverly Connection Shopping Mall

CLIENT:
Beverly Connection Shopping Mall
DESIGNERS:
Constance Beck, Terry P. Graboski
DESIGN FIRM:
Beck & Graboski Design Office
FABRICATOR:
AHR Ampersand
PHOTOGRAPHER:
Terry P. Graboski
MATERIALS:
Fabricated channel letters with exposed neon, internally illuminated cabinets and directories, perforated metals

To create a unifying signage system for a mall complex consisting of two large existing buildings, two new high-tech buildings, a six-cinema complex, a supermarket and a five-level parking structure the designers' theme included a fresh new image and a dashed line connecting graphic shapes between buildings. The signs reflect the crisp architecture with bold clean graphic shapes. The strong colors act as a foil against the raw concrete and muted architectural colors.

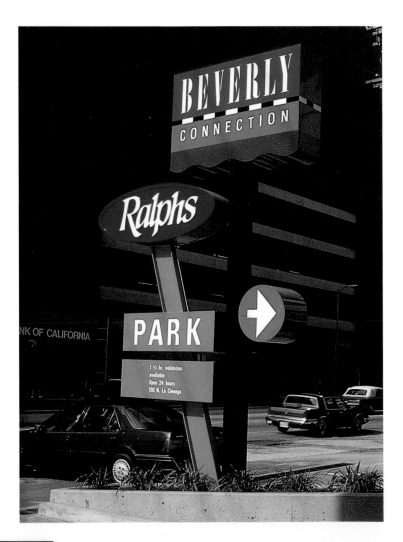

Southland Mall Food Court

CLIENT:
   Equity Properties & Development Company
DESIGNER:
   Tony L. Horton
DESIGN FIRM:
   T L Horton Design, Inc.
FABRICATOR:
   T L Horton Design, Inc.
PHOTOGRAPHER:
   Joe Aker/Aker Photography

Southland Mall's food court in Hayward, California, is highlighted by two 16′ archways identifying the escalators to the festive food court. The signs are outlined in white neon with the new logo in four colors screened on both sides. The columns supporting the signs are made of 12¾″ steel and are powder coated. A metal frame arch above the sign is outlined with white neon and four flags of bent sheet metal top off these entry signs to the food court.

The food court directory is a two-sided transparency box mounted between 8″ posts. The logo and top design complement the identity program created for the entry to the food court. The directory measures 7′ × 4′. All food vendors are included on the sign with beautiful color photography representing the different foods served in the court. The poles are powder coated and the accent colors are latex enamel.

A festive ambience was created with the marquee sign visible to the main level of the court. It is made of plywood and gator foam and the face is 21′ × 9½′. Food Fair is in 24′ letters, 1½″ thick, made of gator foam. The red ribbon spans 150′-wide sheet metal, painted red. Behind the marquee is a 6′-high checked grid made of gator foam. The sign is mounted to the vertical glass and is secured on the single I-beam with piano wire and aircraft cable.

San Francisco Fashion Center

CLIENT:
John Portman and Associates
San Francisco Center
DESIGNER:
Tom Fairclough
DESIGN FIRM:
Primo Angeli Inc.
ART DIRECTOR:
Rolando B. Rosler

The San Francisco Fashion Center includes 550 permanent showrooms and over 100,000 square feet of exhibit space. The signage and graphics have been designed to promote fashion as well as to compliment the architectural design of John Portman and Associates.

Third Street Promenade

CLIENT:
   Bayside District/City of Santa Monica
DESIGNER:
   Noel Davies
DESIGN FIRM:
   Davies Associates
FABRICATOR:
   Windsor Display

A graphics program was implemented as part of the the redevelopment of the Third Street Promenade retail mall in the Bayside District of Santa Monica, California. The program consists of directories, parking directionals, district identity elements and decorative banners.

Larimer Square

CLIENT:
The Hahn Company
LaJolla, California
DESIGN PRINCIPAL:
Henry Beer
DESIGNERS:
Mark Tweed, Phil Reed
PROJECT MANAGER:
Gary Kushner
DESIGN FIRM:
Communication Arts Inc.
ARCHITECT:
Semple Brown Roberts

Communication Arts designed and implemented a new project identity, signing and graphics program for Denver's Larimer Square, a historic downtown commercial district listed on the National Register of Historic Places. The firm designed a family of identities that respect the historic significance of the area while creating a fresh, new look for this downtown retail neighborhood.

Ford City

CLIENT:
  Equity Properties and Development Company
  Chicago, Illinois
DESIGN PRINCIPAL:
  Henry Beer
DESIGNERS:
  Bryan Gough, Nick Igel
PROJECT MANAGER:
  John Ward
DESIGN FIRM:
  Communication Arts Inc.
ARCHITECTS:
  Loebl, Schlossman, and Hackl
PHOTOGRAPHER:
  R. Greg Hursley

Ford City is a 25-year-old, 4,750,000-square-foot mixed-use complex containing 1,650,000 square feet of retail space. The center is an enclosed single-level super regional mall connected by an underground walkway containing 50 specialty shops. Communication Arts designed the interior of the main mall, a new food court, a retail walkway and both new exterior/interior identity graphics for the project.

Cambridgeside Galleria Parking Garage

CLIENT:
Cambridgeside Galleria
DESIGNER:
Robin Perkins
DESIGN FIRM:
Clifford Selbert Design
FABRICATOR:
Design Communications

Cambridgeside Galleria is a shopping mall in Cambridge, Massachusetts, that needed parking directories and signage to assist people in finding their cars in the parking garage. The signage is done in bold colors and made easy by level and numbered section.

Flatbush Avenue Sign Sculpture

CLIENT:
Flatbush Development Corporation
DESIGNERS:
Kenneth Carbone, Leslie Smolan
DESIGN FIRM:
Carbone Smolan Associates
PHOTOGRAPHER:
Kenneth Carbone

Carbone Smolan Associates designed the logotype, sculpture and graphics program for the Flatbush Avenue commercial revitalization.

Los Arcos Mall

CLIENT:
   Equity Properties & Development Company
DESIGNER:
   Tony L. Horton
DESIGN FIRM:
   T L Horton Design, Inc.
PHOTOGRAPHER:
   Joe Aker/Aker Photography

The primary design objective for Los Arcos Mall in Scottsdale, Arizona, was to create a shopping environment that would enhance retail while attracting a broader shopper market and a stronger, more diverse tenant mix. A new food court was added in-line at the front of the main entry. The food court was designed in Santa Fe style with the use of stucco, light colors, natural tile and bleached woods. Blade signage was added to easily identify these in-line stores for shoppers as they walked down the corridor. A new logo applied to decorative signage directed shoppers to this new destination point within the center.

Southgate Plaza

CLIENT:
   Equity Properties & Development Company
DESIGNER:
   Tony L. Horton
DESIGN FIRM:
   T L Horton Design, Inc.
FABRICATOR:
   T L Horton Design, Inc.

The Palm Court, the Southgate Plaza's food court, is identified with this two-sided sign. One side is the identity for the court, one side, a clock. The letters are dimensional and outlined in white neon. White neon also outlines the perimeter of the sign or the plate. Dimensionality is key with each feature of the sign a varied thickness. The sign's colors and patterns complement the center's overall new Floridian deco look.

Columbus Day Sale

CLIENT:
The Hecht Company
Arlington, Virginia
DESIGNER:
Sally Hoffmaster

Taking advantage of the silk-screen process, the designer used the turquoise and creme plate to overprint the black plate. This resulted in a five-color job that looks more like a seven-color job.

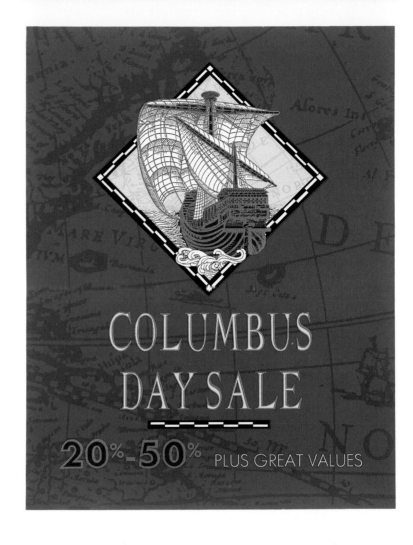

Center Court Clock Sign

CLIENT:
Fox River Mall
Appleton, Wisconsin
DESIGNER:
Tony L. Horton
DESIGN FIRM:
T L Horton Design, Inc.
DEVELOPMENT COMPANY:
The General Growth Companies
Minneapolis, Minnesota
FABRICATOR:
T L Horton Design, Inc.
PHOTOGRAPHER:
Steve Newby/Steve Newby Photogrqaphy

This sign, made as a clock, is positioned to indicate the direction to the food court area. The clock's face is 36" in diameter and the entire sign measures 4' wide. The clock is painted with latex enamel, a palette of five bright colors. A metal fork and knife become the clock's hands.

Sports/Recreational Facilities

Denver Sports Complex

CLIENT:
   City and County of Denver, Parks and Recreation
   Denver, Colorado
DESIGN PRINCIPAL:
   Richard Foy
DESIGNERS:
   Mark Tweed, Phil Reed
PROJECT MANAGER:
   Gary Kushner
DESIGN FIRM:
   Communication Arts Inc.

Communication Arts invented a system of "goal posts" which beckon and orient the visitor, as well as create the boundaries of this urban sports district. This major identification sign is coherent by day, dramatic at dusk, and imparts a sports-like atmosphere. The firm introduced a new color palette, a scoreboard, interior/exterior informational, directional and regulatory signs for the 75,000 seat stadium. The program utilizes durable, low cost materials and finishes which were implemented in phases over a 5-year period by the City of Denver's operations department. The program was completed in 1991.

Madison Square Garden

CLIENT:
Madison Square Garden Corporation
New York, New York
DESIGNERS:
Gary Kushner, Guy Thornton, Bryan Gough
David Shelton, Kevin Kearney, Margaret Sewall
Dave Tweed, Zina Castanuela, Rory McCarthy
Julie Wynn
DESIGN FIRM:
Communication Arts Inc.
ARCHITECTS:
Ellerbe Becket
Kansas City, Missouri
FABRICATORS:
White Way Sign & Maintenance, Clear Corporation
West Side Neon Inc. & Artkraft Strauss Sign Corp.
Rathe Productions, Innoventions, Rosco,
Universal Unlimited
PHOTOGRAPHER:
R. Greg Hursley

To help Madison Square Garden increase ticket sales and events, Communication Arts designed the identity and the interior/environmental signs for the renovation of this historical landmark in New York City. A pattern of lines and a color palette of teal and violet were repeated throughout the signage program to create unity and guide the visitor through one million square feet of space.

To draw people inside the building, a series of 30' identification signs were mounted on Two Penn Plaza, an office tower that hides the Garden's entrance from the street. Channel letters were designed to be transparent during the day and illuminating at night. The letters are mounted against an array of lines that are fabricated of steel tubes and painted metallic gold. The street identifier that attracts the most attention is a new 15' × 35' electronic billboard with a four-color solid-matrix message.

In the directional signs, the violet drop shadows accentuate the white letters.

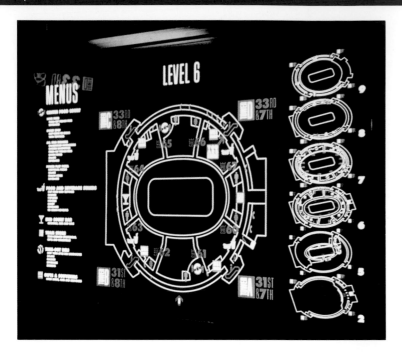

The most expensive and the largest sign for this program was the 16' high and 39' wide center scoreboard. The designers gave this 24-ton board eight sides, including four video screens for instant replay, four scoreboards, four matrix boards and eight rotating panels. The structure raises to the roof for concerts and drops to the floor for maintenance.

Inside the bar, black-and-white photographic images mounted in projecting blades tell animated stories. The images, which are laminated to hard board and covered with clear film for cleaning, slide out of their aluminum channel frames for replacement.

The Play by Play Bar features a 3-D sign which you can walk into. A tapered red "longue" repeats the logo using acrylic letters pushed through the cabinet and is internally illuminated.

Target Center Arena

CLIENT:
Minnesota Timberwolves
Minneapolis, Minnesota
DESIGN PRINCIPAL:
Richard Foy
DESIGNERS:
Mark Tweed, Margaret Sewell
PROJECT MANAGER:
John Ward
DESIGN FIRM:
Communication Arts Inc.
ARCHITECT:
KMR Architects
PHOTOGRAPHERS:
Steven Bergerson, Shin Koyama

The Target Center Arena for the Minnesota Timberwolves opened in 1990. The signage and graphics program encompassed the exterior facade treatment, lower-level lobby, interior signing system, corridor and stair treatment, and concession guidelines.

Stonecreek, The Golf Club

CLIENT:
**Stonecreek, The Golf Club
Phoenix, Arizona**
DESIGNERS:
Jim Bolek, Neill Fox
DESIGN FIRM:
Richardson or Richardson
FABRICATORS:
**Original Rock of Arizona
Case Sandblasting, Arizona**
MATERIALS:
Granulated cement, exterior grade enamels

Identity design and complete Tee-Graphic Signage for an 18-hole Golf Course. All signs for this 18-hole golf course were fabricated off-site of granulated cement. The graphics and typography were hand-cut for sandblasting and then hand painted with exterior grade enamels.

Seven Hills Park

CLIENT:
Somerville, Massachusetts
ART DIRECTOR:
Clifford Selbert
DESIGNER:
Robin Perkins
DESIGN FIRM:
Clifford Selbert Design
SCULPTOR:
Amidon & Company
PHOTOGRAPHER:
Anton Grassl

A series of whimsical sculptural weathervanes is the focus of Seven Hills Park. Symbolizing the original seven hills of Somerville, these environmental graphics animate the city's history and stand as a dynamic civic landmark. The park is a vital community resource—where there was once a parking lot. The sculptures and towers are intended to reflect the railroad line once at this location, as well as to evoke American folk art traditions of weathervanes.

Hotels/Convention Centers

CHAPTER FIVE

Tampa Convention Center

CLIENT:
City of Tampa
Tampa, Florida
DESIGNERS:
Charles P. Reay, Louise W. Angst, Scott Hueting,
Daniel Young, Deborah Beckett, Bevin Grant,
Quintin Richardson
DESIGN FIRM:
Hellmuth, Obata & Kassabaum, Inc.
FABRICATOR:
Offenhauser Company
PHOTOGRAPHER:
HOK Photography

The Tampa Convention Center is located in the downtown area on a river of Tampa Bay. The thematic "wave" and the color blue have been incorporated into the Convention Center logo and building signage, and they appear as accent elements throughout the facility. The wave pattern and central gold-leafed logotype which identifies the two exhibit halls are cast aluminum, and the tesserae mosaic tile work falls approximately three feet behind the metal graphics panel. Each meeting room entry is identified by an open half-round canopy fabricated of cast aluminum. The room numbers appear at the ⅙ point of the circle and are visible from all angles.

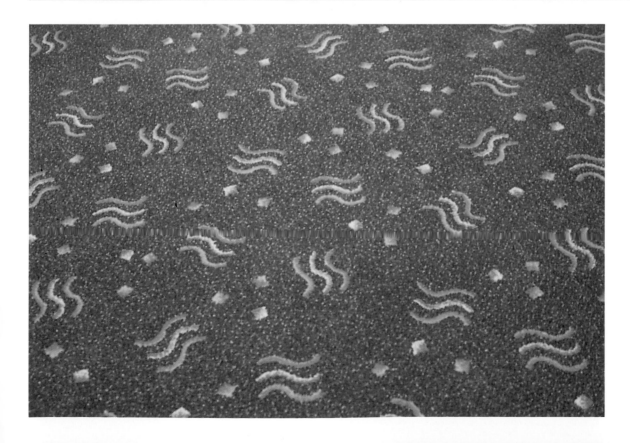

Hollywood Roosevelt Hotel

CLIENT:
   Hollywood Roosevelt Hotel
   Hollywood, California
DESIGN FIRM:
   Beck & Graboski Design Office
FABRICATORS:
   Windsor Displays, Inc. and Architectural Signing Inc.,
   Eric's Creative Wrought Iron
PHOTOGRAPHER:
   Terry P. Graboski

The Hollywood Roosevelt Hotel was opened in 1927 and was the site of the first Academy Awards ceremony which was held in the famed Blossom Room Ballroom. The designers wanted to retain the flavor of the original architecture, yet bring the facility up to first class standards. Directories, meeting room identification signs and other public space information signs were fabricated in polished brass and etched glass. The grand entry gateway was designed in the style of the old Hollywood movie studios with wrought iron, gold leaf detailing and integral lighting fixtures.

↑ Pool
Tropicana Bar
130 - 149
230 - 249
160 - 169

← 101 - 129
201 - 229

Port de Plaisance

CLIENT:
   TESI N.V., Port de Plaisance
DESIGNERS:
   Cynthia Hanegraaf, Rebecca Robin, Elaine Mandeville
ARCHITECTS:
   Edward D. Stone, Jr. and Associates
FABRICATOR:
   SouthWood
MATERIALS:
   Redwood, cast resin room numbers

This sign system was developed for an island resort in the Caribbean. Crafted from wood, the signs convey the impression that they were fabricated locally. The architectural detail and the tropical environment evoke a floral theme.

Morgans Hotel

CLIENT:
Morgans Hotel Group
New York City
DESIGN FIRM:
Tracy Turner Design, Inc.
INTERIOR DESIGN:
Andrée Putman

The designers wanted to create a corporate identity, but without being "corporate." The strong statement made by the interior architecture and details was to carry through on every item. For unity, the type style Helvetica Light in black was used.

The Royalton Hotel

CLIENT:
Morgans Hotel Group
New York City
DESIGN FIRM:
Tracy Turner Design, Inc.
INTERIOR DESIGN:
Philippe Starck

A unique feature of the signage for the Royalton is the lighted sandblasted glass disc that forms a moon-like glow in the dark blue corridors. Helvetica Light in blue was used in the signs to evoke an elegant and warm feeling.

Lodge at Cordillera

CLIENT:
Kensington Land Investment Partners
DESIGN PRINCIPAL:
Richard Foy
DESIGNERS:
Keith Harley, Mark Tweed, Jennifer Harms, Zina Castanuela
DESIGN FIRM:
Communication Arts Inc.
PHOTOGRAPHER:
R. Greg Hursley

Communication Arts designed the custom signage, restaurant identity, guest room collateral and a marketing brochure for the Lodge at Cordillera, a luxury executive retreat west of Vail, Colorado. With only 28 rooms, Cordillera has acres of forest and groomed cross country ski trails. The design goal was to give form to the owner's vision of the qualities of European elegance and Rocky Mountain splendor.

Marriott Courtyard

CLIENT:
Marriott Corporation
DESIGN FIRM:
Lipson-Alport-Glass & Associates
FABRICATOR:
Acme-Wiley

Marriot's welcoming Courtyard sign is metal and plastic fabrication. Internal illumination of the complete sign face effectively projects the design and information after dark.

Restaurants

Nacho Mamma's

CLIENT:
Nacho Mamma's Restaurant
Des Moines, Iowa
DESIGNER:
John Sayles
DESIGN FIRM:
Sayles Graphic Design
FABRICATOR:
Kevin Seiberling
NEON:
Rick Sheridan
PHOTOGRAPHER:
Bill Nellans

The sign is constructed from aluminum and neon. Existing canvas building awnings were hand-painted with co-ordinating graphics. The designer matched the color palette of Nacho Mamma's identity signage with the interior's colors.

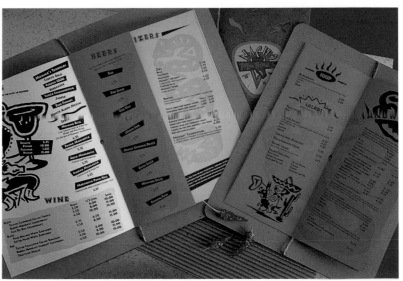

Unlimited Pastabilities

CLIENT:
Paul and Kathy Spadaro
DESIGNERS:
Robert Louey, Regina Rubino
DESIGN FIRMS:
Louey/Rubino Design Group
Tony Chi & Associates
FABRICATOR:
Cival Trovato/P.M. Cousins
PHOTOGRAPHER:
Dub Rogers

The design objective for Unlimited Pastabilities was to create a warm feeling of Mom's Country Kitchen in a busy food court where shoppers and employees take a break for refreshment and quality food in a shopping mall. In order to create the imagery associated with a country kitchen, two scenes were developed. The main focal point is a country table in the center with two counters on either side. The second scene is an open kitchen with a black gunmetal hood above a terra cotta-tiled cooking counter below and curly maple cabinetry behind. The introduction of a traditional white tile pattern with black mosaic inserts and alternating custom hand-painted tile depicting the logo are used both in the foreground as wainscotting and on the rear wall and back splash as a backdrop. This traditional tile pattern and other artifacts depicting images of home cooking dispel the cold scenery of the shopping mall and set the stage for a relaxed dining experience.

UNLIMITED PASTABILITIES

HOMEMADE ITALIAN SOUPS	TAKE HOME— FRESH ITALIAN SAUCES
Chicken over noodles 3.95	"OUR MARINARA" 5.7
Beans w/ Ditellini 3.95	"OUR meat" 6.2
(Fagioli)	
Lentil + Escarole 3.95	

BREAD	
Garlic	75¢
Italian Toast	50¢
Italian Bread Toast	2.25

FRESH PASTA—(uncooked)
BY THE POUND

dinners	6.25
Chicken Cutlet Parm Platter	
Eggplant Parm. Platter	6.00

Egg Pasta	2.15
Tomato Pasta	3.00
Spinach Pasta	3.25
Whole Wheat	3.75

The Silver Diner

CLIENT:
The Silver Diner
DESIGNERS:
Charles Morris Mount, David Ramos
DESIGN FIRM:
Silver & Ziskind/Mount
FABRICATOR:
Belsinger Sign Works, Inc.
PHOTOGRAPHER:
Doug Brown

With glowing neon messages, the exterior signage for The Silver Diner leads the visitor into a nostalgic journey. A 26′ high glass block tower functions as a signpost and is the base for a 6′ high red and blue neon clock. Two tubes of blue neon in custom stainless steel channels replicate the log. "Silver Diner" is supported by three stainless steel channels illuminated by red neon and attached to the facade of the tower on either side of the glass block. The clock's finish is baked enamel trimmed in blue neon and the tag line is in red neon letters.

Off the Wall Cafe

CLIENT:
Apple Computer, Inc.
DESIGN FIRM:
Profile Design
ART DIRECTOR:
Thomas McNulty
FABRICATORS:
Alan Wolf/California Model and Design
Tony Erpelding/Erpelding Design
MATERIALS:
Plexiglas, sheet metals, neon lighting

Designed with three-dimensional tables hanging from the walls and classic black and white posters brightened with blue neon lights, the Off the Wall Cafe identity and environmental signage communicates an exciting and original atmosphere for Apple employees within a corporate structure.

Mega • Bite Cafe

CLIENT:
   Apple Computer, Inc.
DESIGNER:
   Thomas McNulty
DESIGN FIRM:
   Profile Design
FABRICATORS:
   Alan Wolf/California Model and Design
   Tony Erpelding/Erpelding
MATERIALS:
   Plexiglas, sheet metals and neon lighting

Identity for Mega • Bite, an employee cafe at Apple Computer, is designed to speak to a technical audience. The humanized "Mega Man" serves as a mascot for the cafe which creates a dynamic and memorable environment for Apple employees.

Tech Talk Cafe

CLIENT:
   Apple Computer, Inc.
DESIGNER:
   Thomas McNulty
DESIGN FIRM:
   Profile Design
FABRICATORS:
   Alan Wolf/California Model and Design
   Tony Erpelding/Erpelding Design
MATERIALS:
   Plexiglas, neon lighting and metal holding brackets

The Tech Talk Cafe identity and environmental signage connotes time and place. Using a clock as the central theme, the identity system comunicates its message in a creative and distinctive manner.

147

Valeriano's Ristorante

CLIENT:
 Valeriano's Ristorante
 Los Gatos, California
DESIGNERS:
 Rick Tharp, Jana Heer, Kim Tomlinson
DESIGN FIRM:
 THARP DID IT
FABRICATORS:
 Muscato Signs
PHOTOGRAPHER:
 Kelly O'Connor
MATERIALS:
 The signage above the main entry is fabricated of a lightweight foam and faux painted. Window signs are hand painted and gold leafed.

Rick Tharp wanted the signage for Valeriano's Ristorante to look as though it had always been there. He designed the logo to capture the mood of the restaurant; eclectic, old-world and very Italian. The building was built in the mid-1800s and was the original Bank of Italy in Los Gatos, California. Originally named "Il Nido," meaning the nest, the restaurant moved from its upstairs location to the ground level and changed its name to Valeriano's, taken from the owner's name. In order to retain customer recognition, the designers suggested incorporating the original name as a permanent element of the logo in the window signage.

Blackhawk Grille

CLIENT:
  California Restaurant Group
DESIGNERS:
  Rick Tharp, Jana Heer, Jean Mogannam, Kim Tomlinson
DESIGN FIRM:
  THARP DID IT
FABRICATOR:
  Eclipse, Russ Williams
INTERIOR DESIGN:
  Engstrom & Hofling

This restaurant is located near a classic car museum. A different auto is featured in the bar area each month. Subtle references to automotive technology and eclectic design elements were combined with a deco logotype to hearken back to a bygone era of automotive history.

The wall sconces are actual hubcaps detailed with the "BG" ligature. The light source is concealed behind them. The wine-by-the glass board was fabricated from a sheet of galvanized aluminum so that wines could be changed daily by using a dry wipe marker. The logo and ruled lines were silk-screened on the face. The frame was built into the wall and covered with the same handmade paper covering as the walls. Rick Tharp wanted it to appear as architectural articulation rather than an add-on sign. The host station is built of wood with a back-lit aluminum face plate with the ligature cut out. A piece of Plexiglas is mounted behind it to allow soft light diffusion.

News Bar

CLIENT:
 News Bar
 New York City
DESIGN FIRM:
 Tracy Turner Design, Inc.
ARCHITECT:
 Wayne Turett

The designers developed the graphics program for this new coffee bar and newsstand in the heart of the Flat Iron district. This included the logo, signage, menu boards, bookmarks and t-shirts.

Tutto Mare

CLIENT:
  Spectrum Foods, Inc.
ART DIRECTOR:
  Judi Radice
DESIGN FIRM:
  Primo Angeli, Inc.
FABRICATOR:
  HowenSign
PHOTOGRAPHER:
  Beatriz Coll
MATERIALS:
  Reverse channel letters with a coral tinted gel cast a
  halo effect on the wall. The returns of the letters were
  painted to resemble patina.

Tutto Mare, a contemporary Italian restaurant with an
emphasis on seafood, is located in the Fashion Island
Center of Newport Beach, California. The designers
wanted to create a sign treatment that would look good
in the daylight as well as draw attention to the location at
night. The architect, inspired by the logo design, used
the "serpentine" motif as door handles.

Pizza Connection

CLIENT:
  Kingston Pizburg Associates
DESIGNERS:
  Tony Chi, Albert Chen, Rafael Caceres Jr.
DESIGN FIRM:
  Tony Chi & Associates
GRAPHIC DESIGN:
  The Marketing Partnership
FABRICATOR:
  R.J. Reardon Construction Co., Inc.
PHOTOGRAPHER:
  Dub Rogers
MATERIALS:
  Gypsum wall board, neon tube, stainless steel letters,
  stainless steel frame with silk screening

Pizza Connection is a pizza bar located in the food court
of Independence Mall at Kingston, Massachusetts. Its
design creates a futuristic and dominant image with a
striking color contrast which grasps the customer's attention. The conventional bulkhead is set back to create
a niche for dispensing the pizza. The logo and menu
board within this niche is highlighted with four giant tri-
angular torchiers. To create a powerful image, the rear
kitchen and the storage area are concealed by the sym-
metrical storefront.

Cultural/Educational Institutions

RCH

sity of Colorado

Clark College Library Foundation

CLIENT:
Clark College Library Foundation
Vancouver, Washington
DESIGN DIRECTOR:
Kenneth G. Ambrosini
PROJECT MANAGER:
Richard A. Gottfried
DESIGN FIRM:
Design Partnership
FABRICATOR:
Savoy Studios
PHOTOGRAPHER:
Todd Eckelman Photography
MATERIALS:
Acid etched, canyon-cut aniline died, sandblasted and drilled laminated glass, solid maple stock, steel hex head fasteners, solid stock plate steel

Instead of traditional bronze cast plaques to commemorate and recognize the donors for Clark College's new library, the designers used a sculpture of carved and etched glass that reflected the library's major commissioned art piece. The design goal was to create a piece that would attract attention, could change its personality as the light conditions fluctuated within the space, could stand alone as a piece of art and yet would not appear as an intrusion within the space, had permanence and would give recognition to the conributors.

The Pierpont Morgan Library

CLIENT:
The Pierpont Morgan Library
DESIGNERS:
Kenneth Carbone, Beth Bangor
DESIGN FIRM:
Carbone Smolan Associates
PHOTOGRAPHER:
Paul Warchol

The signage program for The Pierpont Morgan Library includes orientation maps, directional signs, gallery identification, code signage and benefactor's identification. The signs are made of red brass with three kinds of special custom Patina finish that was hand applied on a custom textural background.

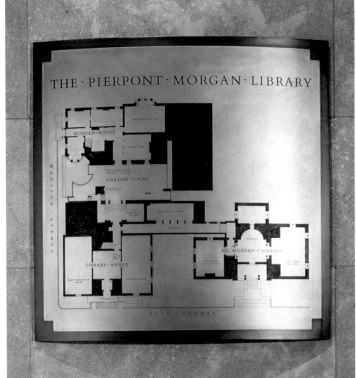

The Ronald Reagan Presidential Library

CLIENT:
**Reagan Presidential Foundation
Simi Valley, California**
DESIGNERS:
**Nancye Green, Susan Berman, Alexis Cohen, Alan Ford
Gabrielle Goodman, Robert Henry, Adrian Levin
Susan Myers, Patrick Nolan, Allen Wilpon**
DESIGN FIRM:
Donovan & Green
FABRICATOR:
**Peerless Woodworking/The Larkworthy Group
Signs and Decal**
MATERIALS:
**Lacquered wood, silkscreening, photographic
reproduction, etched and filled steel, etched and
filled bronze**

The "Hall of the Presidents" Gallery features cut-out bronze signatures of the 39 presidents preceding Ronald Reagan with their terms of office indicated below. Anigre wood veneer walls form the enclosure of this gallery. Ronald Reagan's cut-out bronze signature is placed on a back-lit glass wall on which the presidential seal is sandblasted.

A steel-panelled wall in the "Voices of Freedom" Gallery lists the names of dissidents from around the world. Artifacts and photos from individuals persecuted for their political and religious beliefs are displayed in cases. The stories of each featured person are silk-screened on steel plaques.

University of Colorado Research Park

CLIENT:
**University of Colorado
Boulder, Colorado**
DESIGN PRINCIPAL:
Richard Foy
DESIGNERS:
Phil Reed, Patty Van Hook
PROJECT MANAGER:
Gary Kushner
DESIGN FIRM:
Communication Arts Inc.
ARCHITECT:
Gage Davis International

Communication Arts developed the overall signage and identity, including the directional and informational signage for this new high-tech research facility owned by the University of Colorado. Entry signs and sculptures were carved from local stone, etched with gold leaf and depict scientific and mathematical symbols.

The Louvre Visitor Information System and Sign Program

CLIENT:
The Louvre
DESIGN DIRECTOR:
Kenneth Carbone
DESIGNERS:
**John Plunkett, Barbara Kuhr, Beth Bangor
Claire Taylor, Erik Pike**
DESIGN FIRM:
Carbone Smolan Associates
DESIGN IMPLEMENTATION:
Architecture Design Societe Anonyme
CONSULTANT:
Dominique Pierzo
ASSISTANT:
Lise Andrault
PHOTOGRAPHERS:
Phillipe de Potestad, George Kamper

The visitor information system and sign program for Etablissement Public du Grand Louvre in Paris, France, included hand-carved letters in marble, glass and stainless steel directional signs, aluminum and silk-screen orientation maps, and bead-blast stainless steel letters. The typeface used throughout the program is granjon with universe as a secondary typeface. A tri-color coding system is used for vertical circulation. The program is in French only with a numerical coding system for orientation. This system is directly linked to a paper guide available upon admission in six individual languages.

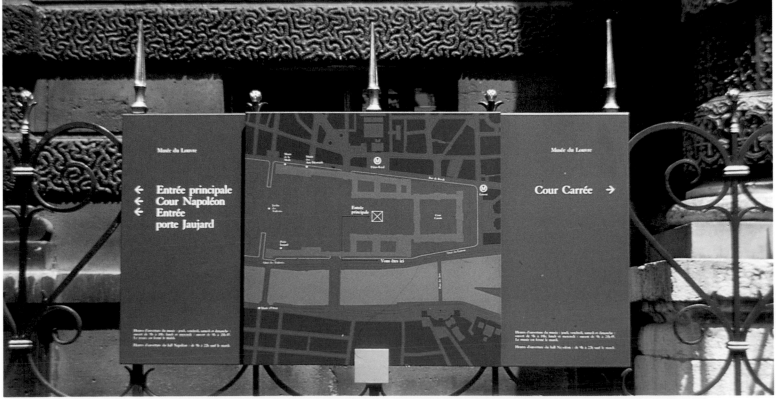

Pavilion for Japanese Art

CLIENT:
  Los Angeles County Museum of Art
PROJECT MANAGER:
  Terry P. Graboski
DESIGN DIRECTOR:
  Constance Beck
DESIGN FIRM:
  Beck & Graboski
ARCHITECT:
  Bruce Goff
FABRICATOR:
  AHR Ampersand
PHOTOGRAPHER:
  Terry P. Graboski

A logo was created to symbolize the building shape, and is used on glass as line of site barriers and as I.D. tags on various signs. The donor wall in the style of a Japanese screen is made of zig zag aluminum cantilevered off a curved wall. The background is gold leaf to reflect the traditional use of gold in Japanese art and is covered with ⅜″ glass panels with deep etched and paint filled copy. All panels are hinged. The art identification signs are mounted on an acrylic holder that is fastened to the clear hand rail with brushed brass clips.

The Board of Trustees of the
Los Angeles County Museum of Art
gratefully acknowledges the generosity
of the following donors to the Campaign
for the Pavilion for Japanese Art:

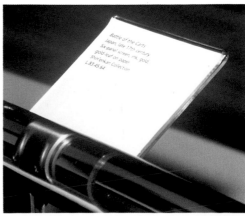

Museum of Modern Art

CLIENT:
Museum of Modern Art
New York, New York
DESIGNER:
Kenneth Carbone
DESIGN FIRM:
Carbone Smolan Associates
PHOTOGRAPHER:
Mark Greenburg

This signage program for the Museum of Art includes exterior and interior architectural signs for the galleries, book store, auditorium, restaurant and major public spaces. Various sign components include fiberglass panels with stainless steel letters, banners, glass poster displays and multi-colored signs for the museum's cafe.

Peabody Museum Asian Export Art Wing

CLIENT:
  Peabody Museum of Salem
DESIGNERS:
  **Michael Donovan, Susan Berman, Robert Henry,
  Lori Hom**
DESIGN FIRM:
  Donovan & Green
FABRICATOR:
  Rathe Productions
PHOTOGRAPHER:
  Wolfgang Hoyt
MATERIALS:
  Lacquered wood, plexiglass, silkscreening

The Peabody Museum of Salem, America's oldest continuously operating museum, added a wing for the display of Asian Export Art. The designs developed for the galleries include displays for the objects as well as extensive visual and graphic interpretive materials, including silkscreened graphics that utilize traditional Chinese, Japanese, and Indian design motifs. There is a balanced presentation of the objects that creates appropriately scaled, elegant settings while also providing an historical overview and context for appreciating the collection.

The John F. Kennedy Center for the Performing Arts

CLIENT:
The John F. Kennedy Center for the Performing Arts
Washington, D.C.
DESIGNERS:
Kathleen W. Herring
Nichols • Dezenhall Communications
Management Group
Peter Van Allen
Creative Signage Systems
DESIGN FIRM:
Nichols • Dezenhall Communications
Management Group
FABRICATOR:
Cornelius Architectural Products
PHOTOGRAPHER:
Earl Zubkoff

The signs were designed to help visitors find their way to the two ticket offices, five theaters and three restaurants located in the Kennedy Center from a variety of entry points. Directional information is displayed on 84″ × 30″ × 30″ freestanding primary kiosks clad with black laminate graphics, hydrocut brass mirror polished faces and edges.

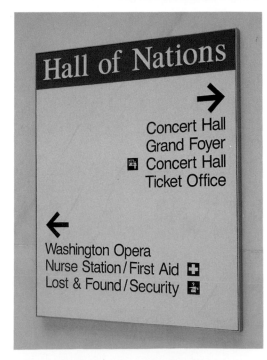

Carnegie Hall

CLIENT:
   Carnegie Hall
   New York, New York
DESIGN FIRM:
   Tracy Turner Design, Inc.

Working on the renovation and restoration of Carnegie Hall, the designers and architects maintained a clear respect for the architecture by using traditional materials such as glass, burnished and unburnished gold leaf, and bronze. The designers incorporated elements used throughout the architectural design as design motifs for use on the signage border designs. The wreath motif from the front facade of the building was developed as a decorative design element for use on the mirror frames and the donor plaques. To provide continuity, the type face, Goudy Old Style, was used as the sign standard for the Hall since this was already being used for Carnegie Hall's marketing and promotional materials. The burgundy color used for the signage was consistent with the interior's scheme and in use by the Hall on other printed matter.

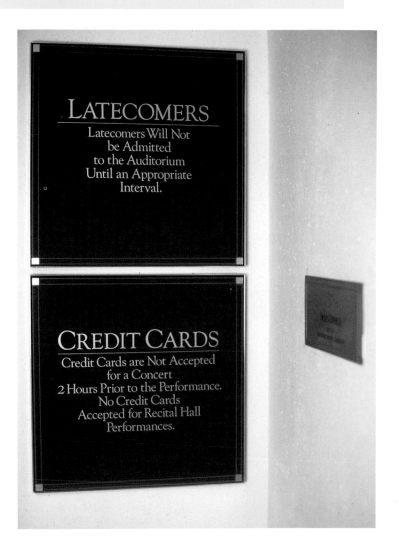

STAIRS TO ALL LEVELS

◄ FIRST TIER
◄ SECOND TIER
Restrooms
▶ LOWER LEVEL
Restrooms

SECOND TIER

New York Botanical Garden

CLIENT:
   New York Botanical Garden
DESIGNER:
   Linda Konda
DESIGN FIRM:
   Clifford Selbert Design
   Cambridge, Massachusetts
ILLUSTRATORS:
   Paul Ritscher, Bruce Hutchinson, Daniel Craig
FABRICATOR:
   Design Communications
PHOTOGRAPHER:
   Anton Grassl

The designer implemented environmental graphics into the signage program for the world's second largest botanical garden. In the garden, information and maps are displayed on pylon kiosks. Floral and informational banners grace the building's exterior.

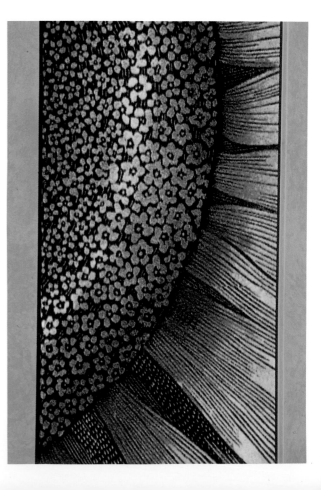

Jungle of the Apes

CLIENT:
  St. Louis Zoological Park
  Forest Park
  St. Louis, Missouri
DESIGNERS:
  Charles P. Reay, Louise W. Grant, Bevin Grant,
  Theresa Henriken, Aen Reay, Greg Youngstrom
DESIGN FIRM:
  Hellmuth, Obata & Kassabaum, Inc.
FABRICATORS:
  ASI Sign Systems, Inc.; Don Ashbee, Blacksmith, Inc.;
  Enameltec
PHOTOGRAPHER:
  HOK Photography

The area identification sign is a forged and hammered steel replica of the logo and modified Gil Sans typography handcrafted by a blacksmith artisan. This sign is supported by natural 10″ diameter wood poles set into the berm surrounding the building. The exterior free-standing display panels combine text, photography, illustration and charts to describe the forms and behaviors of the animals in relation to their natural context. They cover topics such as habitat, community, physiology, threats to survival and causes of endangerment.

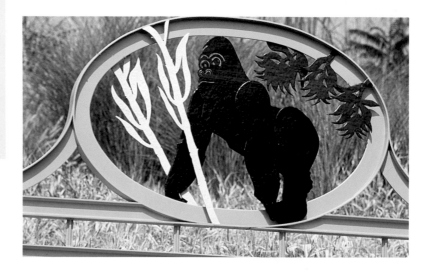

The murals
were made possible by
the generosity of
Mildred Goodwin
in memory of her mother
Ann Wendell

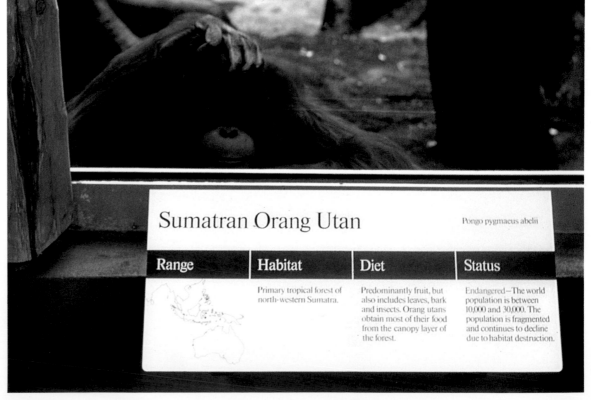

Sumatran Orang Utan

Pongo pygmaeus abelii

Range	Habitat	Diet	Status
	Primary tropical forest of north-western Sumatra.	Predominantly fruit, but also includes leaves, bark and insects. Orang utans obtain most of their food from the canopy layer of the forest.	Endangered—The world population is between 10,000 and 30,000. The population is fragmented and continues to decline due to habitat destruction.

These Field Notes describe Gorilla behavior in the wild.

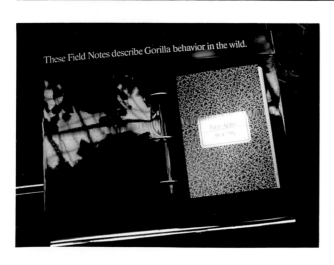

These Field Notes describe Gorilla behavior in the wild.

The Living World

CLIENT:
   St. Louis Zoological Park
   Forest Park
   St. Louis, Missouri
DESIGNERS:
   Director: Charles P. Reay
   Manager: Louise W. Angst
   Designers: Bevin Grant, Theresa Henrekin
DESIGN FIRM:
   Hellmuth, Obata & Kassabaum, Inc.
FABRICATORS:
   Crampton, Inc.
   ASI Sign Systems, Inc.
PHOTOGRAPHERS:
   Burt Glinn, Robert Pettus, George Cott,
   HOK Photography

The Living World building is identified by porcelain enamel letters that are representations of animal skin patterns—tiger, leopard, python, butterfly, zebra and giraffe. The "O" in the the word "World" is represented by a globe.

On the interior, a painted metal armature suspended from light standards, symmetrically circles the rotunda and contains the major directional and hall identification signage. Life-size fiberglass sculptures are suspended from the ceiling.

A fiberglass directory is mounted to the rotunda handrail. All major areas are simply represented and clearly identified by blocks of color related to their function.

Medical Facilities

CHAPTER EIGHT

Oak Park Hospital

CLIENT:
Oak Park Hospital
Oak Park, Illinois
DESIGN FIRM:
PlanCom, Inc.
FABRICATOR:
Poblocki Sign Systems
MATERIALS:
Aluminum, lexian, acrylic

The goal was to design a wayfinding system that allows the 300-bed hospital to be traveled quickly and to provide minimal environmental disturbance, while at the same time offering maximum legibility, clear information and flexibility. The designers developed appropriate traffic patterns for all areas and plotted the various sign types according to the categories of identification, direction, regulation and information.

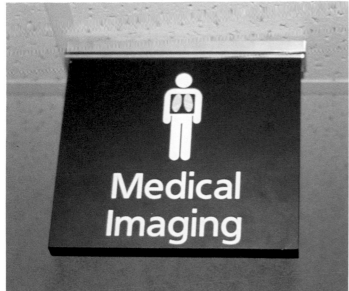

The MetroHealth System

CLIENT:
The MetroHealth System
DESIGNERS:
Karen Skunta, Gerhard Ade
DESIGN FIRM:
Ade Skunta and Company
FABRICATOR:
Simon Signs of Cleveland, Ohio
PHOTOGRAPHER:
Don Snyder
MATERIALS:
Heavy-gauge aluminum, white Plexiglas, epoxy paint

The 8' square sign employs the corporate logo in a three-dimensional form. Fabricated in heavy-gauge aluminum, there are no visible fastenings—all corners and seams are continuously welded and ground smooth. The typography is routed out of the aluminum face and backed with white Plexiglas for night illumination. The free-standing sign is finished in special epoxy paint mixed to match the logo colors.

Addison Design Consultants
575 Sutter St.
San Francisco, CA 94102

Ade Skunta & Company
700 W. St. Clair Ave.
The Hoyt Block
Suite 318
Cleveland, OH 44113

Austin Cline Advertising
304 S. Willow
Tampa, FL 33606

Barry Brothers
1922 E. 18th St.
Brooklyn, NY 11229

Beck & Graboski Design
247 Sixteenth St.
Santa Monica, CA 90402

Biesek Design
2829 Lee Canyon Rd.
San Luis Obispo, CA 93405

Calori & Vanden-Eynden
130 West 25th St.
New York, NY 10001

Carbone Smolan Associates
22 West 19th St.
New York, NY 10011

Clifford Selbert Design
2067 Massachusetts Ave.
3rd Floor
Cambridge, MA 02140

Communication Arts
Incorporated
112 Pearl St.
Boulder, CO 80302-5196

Davies Associates
5817 Uplander Way
Culver City, CA 90230

Design Partnership
500 NW Ninth St.
Portland, OR 97209

Donovan & Green
1 Madison Ave.
39th Floor
New York, NY 10010

Edward D. Stone, Jr.
& Associates
1512 E. Broward Blvd. #110
Ft. Lauderdale, FL 33301

Farrington Design Group
3520 Piedmont Rd. NE
Suite 450
Atlanta, GA 30305

Fitch RichardsonSmith
10350 Olentangy River Rd.
P.O. Box 360
Worthington, OH 43085

The Hecht Company
685 N. Glebe Rd.
Arlington, VA 22203

Hellmuth Obata & Kassabaum
1831 Chestnut St.
St. Louis, MO 63103

Jacoby Reese Design
307 West 200 South
Suite 4005
Salt Lake City, UT 84101

Judi Radice Design Consultant
P.O. Box 26710
San Francisco, CA 94126

Larsen Design Office
7101 York Ave. South
Minneapolis, MN 55435

Lipson Alport Glass
666 Dundee Rd. #103
Northbrook, IL 60062

Louey/Rubino Design
2525 Main St.
Santa Monica, CA 90405

Mike Quon Design Office
568 Broadway
Suite 703
New York, NY 10012

Nichols • Dezenhall
648 Sheridan Rd.
Evanston, IL 60202

The Office of Reginald Wade Richey
1900 Grant St. #840
Denver, CO 80203

Pangborn Design Ltd.
275 Iron St.
Detroit, MI 48207

Plancom, Inc.
542 S. Dearborn St.
Chicago, IL 60605

Primo Angeli Inc.
590 Folsom St.
San Francisco, CA 94105

Profile Design
151 Townsend St.
San Francisco, CA 94107

Richardson or Richardson
1301 E. Bethany Home Rd.
Phoenix, AZ 85014

Sayles Graphic Design
308 8th St.
Des Moines, IA 50309

Silver & Ziskind/Mount
233 Park Ave South
New York, NY 10003

THARP DID IT
50 University Ave. #21
Los Gatos, CA 95030

T L Horton Design
11120 Grader St.
Dallas, TX 75238

Tony Chi Design
611 Broadway
Suite 724
New York, NY 10012

Tracy Turner Design, Inc.
30 W. 22nd St.
New York, NY 10010

Projects

INDEX

Designers

Design Firms